The War That Will End War

H. G. Wells

Alpha Editions

This edition published in 2024

ISBN 9789364732505

Design and Setting By
Alpha Editions
www.alphaedis.com
Email - info@alphaedis.com

As per information held with us this book is in Public Domain.
This book is a reproduction of an important historical work.
Alpha Editions uses the best technology to reproduce historical work
in the same manner it was first published to preserve its original nature.
Any marks or number seen are left intentionally to preserve.

Contents

I	- 1 -
II	- 5 -
III	- 9 -
IV	- 14 -
V	- 18 -
VI	- 23 -
VII	- 28 -
VIII	- 33 -
IX	- 38 -
X	- 43 -
XI	- 47 -

I
WHY BRITAIN WENT TO WAR
A CLEAR EXPOSITION OF WHAT WE ARE FIGHTING FOR

The cause of a war and the object of a war are not necessarily the same. The cause of this war was the invasion of Luxemburg and Belgium. We declared war because we were bound by treaty to declare war. We have been pledged to protect the integrity of Belgium since the kingdom of Belgium has existed. If the Germans had not broken the guarantees they shared with us to respect the neutrality of these little States we should certainly not be at war at the present time. The fortified eastern frontier of France could have been held against any attack without any help from us. We had no obligations and no interests there. We were pledged to France simply to protect her from a naval attack by sea, but the Germans had already given us an undertaking not to make such an attack. It was our Belgian treaty and the sudden outrage on Luxemburg that precipitated us into this conflict. No Power in the world would have respected our Flag or accepted our national word again if we had not fought. So much for the immediate cause of the war.

But now we come to the object of this war. We began to fight because our honour and our pledge obliged us; but so soon as we are embarked upon the fighting we have to ask ourselves what is the end at which our fighting aims. We cannot simply put the Germans back over the Belgian border and tell them not to do it again. We find ourselves at war with that huge military empire with which we have been doing our best to keep the peace since first it rose upon the ruins of French Imperialism in 1871. And war is mortal conflict. We have now either to destroy or be destroyed. We have not sought this reckoning, we have done our utmost to avoid it; but now that it has been forced upon us it is imperative that it should be a thorough reckoning. This is a war that touches every man and every home in each of the combatant countries. It is a war, as Mr. Sidney Low has said, not of soldiers but of whole peoples. And it is a war that must be fought to such a finish that every man in each of the nations engaged understands what has happened. There can be no diplomatic settlement that will leave German Imperialism free to explain away its failure to its people and start new preparations. We have to go on until we are absolutely done for, or until the Germans as a people know that they are beaten, and are convinced that they have had enough of war.

We are fighting Germany. But we are fighting without any hatred of the German people. We do not intend to destroy either their freedom or their unity. But we have to destroy an evil system of government and the mental and material corruption that has got hold of the German imagination and taken possession of German life. We have to smash the Prussian Imperialism as thoroughly as Germany in 1871 smashed the rotten Imperialism of Napoleon III. And also we have to learn from the failure of that victory to avoid a vindictive triumph.

This Prussian Imperialism has been for forty years an intolerable nuisance in the earth. Ever since the crushing of the French in 1871 the evil thing has grown and cast its spreading shadow over Europe. Germany has preached a propaganda of ruthless force and political materialism to the whole uneasy world. "Blood and iron," she boasted, was the cement of her unity, and almost as openly the little, mean, aggressive statesmen and professors who have guided her destinies to this present conflict have professed cynicism and an utter disregard of any ends but nationally selfish ends, as though it were religion. Evil just as much as good may be made into a Cant. Physical and moral brutality has indeed become a cant in the German mind, and spread from Germany throughout the world. I could wish it were possible to say that English and American thought had altogether escaped its corruption. But now at last we shake ourselves free and turn upon this boasting wickedness to rid the world of it. The whole world is tired of it. And "Gott!"—Gott so perpetually invoked—Gott indeed must be very tired of it.

This is already the vastest war in history. It is war not of nations, but of mankind. It is a war to exorcise a world-madness and end an age.

And note how this Cant of public rottenness has had its secret side. The man who preaches cynicism in his own business transactions had better keep a detective and a cash register for his clerks; and it is the most natural thing in the world to find that this system, which is outwardly vile, is also inwardly rotten. Beside the Kaiser stands the firm of Krupp, a second head to the State; on the very steps of the throne is the armament trust, that organised scoundrelism which has, in its relentless propaganda for profit, mined all the security of civilisation, brought up and dominated a Press, ruled a national literature, and corrupted universities.

Consider what the Germans have been, and what the Germans can be. Here is a race which has for its chief fault docility and a belief in teachers and rulers. For the rest, as all who know it intimately will testify, it is the most amiable of peoples. It is naturally kindly, comfort-loving, child-loving, musical, artistic, intelligent. In countless respects German homes and towns and countrysides are the most civilised in the world. But these people did a little lose their heads after the victories of the sixties and seventies, and there began a propaganda of national vanity and national ambition. It was organised by a stupidly forceful statesman, it was fostered by folly upon the throne. It was guarded from wholesome criticism by an intolerant censorship. It never gave sanity a chance. A certain patriotic sentimentality lent itself only too readily to the suggestion of the flatterer, and so there grew up this monstrous trade in weapons. German patriotism became an "interest," the greatest of the "interests." It developed a vast advertisement propaganda. It subsidised Navy Leagues and Aerial Leagues, threatening the world. Mankind, we saw too late, had been guilty of an incalculable folly in permitting private men to make a profit out of the dreadful preparations for war. But the evil was started; the German imagination was captured and enslaved. On every other European country that valued its integrity there was thrust the overwhelming necessity to arm and drill—and still to arm and drill. Money was withdrawn from education, from social progress, from business enterprise, and art and scientific research, and from every kind of happiness; life was drilled and darkened.

So that the harvest of this darkness comes now almost as a relief, and it is a grim satisfaction in our discomforts that we can at last look across the roar and torment of battlefields to the possibility of an organised peace.

For this is now a war for peace.

It aims straight at disarmament. It aims at a settlement that shall stop this sort of thing for ever. Every soldier who fights against Germany now is a crusader against war. This, the greatest of all wars, is not just another war—it is the last war! England, France, Italy, Belgium, Spain, and all the little countries of Europe, are heartily sick of war; the Tsar has expressed a passionate hatred of war; the most of Asia is unwarlike; the United States has no illusions about war. And never was war begun so joyously, and never was war begun with so grim a resolution. In England, France, Belgium, Russia, there is no thought of glory.

We know we face unprecedented slaughter and agonies; we know that for neither side will there be easy triumphs or prancing victories. Already, in that warring sea of men, there is famine as well as hideous butchery, and soon there must come disease.

Can it be otherwise?

We face, perhaps, the most awful winter that mankind has ever faced.

But we English and our allies, who did not seek this catastrophe, face it with anger and determination rather than despair.

Through this war we have to march, through pain, through agonies of the spirit worse than pain, through seas of blood and filth. We English have not had things kept from us. We know what war is; we have no delusions. We have read books that tell us of the stench of battlefields, and the nature of wounds, books that Germany suppressed and hid from her people. And we face these horrors to make an end of them.

There shall be no more Kaisers, there shall be no more Krupps, we are resolved. That foolery shall end!

And not simply the present belligerents must come into the settlement.

All America, Italy, China, the Scandinavian Powers, must have a voice in the final readjustment, and set their hands to the ultimate guarantees. I do not mean that they need fire a single shot or load a single gun. But they must come in. And in particular to the United States do we look to play a part in that pacification of the world for which our whole nation is working, and for which, by the thousand, men are now laying down their lives.

II
THE SWORD OF PEACE
"EVERY SWORD THAT IS DRAWN AGAINST GERMANY NOW IS A SWORD DRAWN FOR PEACE"

Europe is at war!

The monstrous vanity that was begotten by the easy victories of '70 and '71 has challenged the world, and Germany prepares to reap the harvest Bismarck sowed. That trampling, drilling foolery in the heart of Europe, that has arrested civilisation and darkened the hopes of mankind for forty years. German Imperialism, German militarism, has struck its inevitable blow. The victory of Germany will mean the permanent enthronement of the War God over all human affairs. The defeat of Germany may open the way to disarmament and peace throughout the earth.

To those who love peace there can be no other hope in the present conflict than the defeat, the utter discrediting of the German legend, the ending for good and all of the blood and iron superstition, of Krupp, flag-wagging Teutonic Kiplingism, and all that criminal, sham efficiency that centres in Berlin. Never was war so righteous as war against Germany now. Never has any State in the world so clamoured for punishment.

But be it remembered that Europe's quarrel is with the German State, not with the German people; with a system, and not with a race. The older tradition of Germany is a pacific and civilising tradition. The temperament of the mass of German people is kindly, sane and amiable. Disaster to the German Army, if it is unaccompanied by any such memorable wrong as dismemberment or intolerable indignity, will mean the restoration of the greatest people in Europe to the fellowship of Western nations. The *rôle* of England in this huge struggle is plain as daylight. We have to fight. If only on account of the Luxemburg outrage we have to fight. If we do not fight, England will cease to be a country to be proud of; it will be a dirt-bath to escape from. But it is inconceivable that we should not fight. And having fought, then in the hour of victory it will be for us to save the liberated Germans from vindictive treatment, to secure for this great people their right, as one united German-speaking State, to a place in the sun.

First we have to save ourselves and Europe, and then we have to stand between German on the one hand and the Cossack and revenge on the other.

For my own part, I do not doubt that Germany and Austria are doomed to defeat in this war. It may not be catastrophic defeat, though even that is possible, but it is defeat. There is no destiny in the stars and every sign is false if this is not so.

They have provoked an overwhelming combination of enemies. They have under-rated France. They are hampered by a bad social and military tradition. The German is not naturally a good soldier; he is orderly and obedient, but he is not nimble nor quick-witted; since his sole considerable military achievement, his not very lengthy march to Paris in 1870 and '71, the conditions of modern warfare have been almost completely revolutionised and in a direction that subordinates the massed fighting of unintelligent men to the rapid initiative of individualised soldiers. And, on the other hand, since those years of disaster, the Frenchman has learnt the lesson of humility; he is prepared now sombrely for a sombre struggle; his is the gravity that precedes astonishing victories. In the air, in the open field, with guns and machines, it is doubtful if anyone fully realises the superiority of his quality to the German. This sudden attack may take him aback for a week or so, though I doubt even that, but in the end I think he will hold his own; even without us he will hold his own, and with us then I venture to prophesy that within three months from now his Tricolour will be over the Rhine. And even suppose his line gets broken by the first rush. Even then I do not see how the Germans are to get to Paris or anywhere near Paris. I do not see how against the strength of the modern defensive and the stinging power of an intelligent enemy in retreat, of which we had a little foretaste in South Africa, the exploit of Sedan can be repeated. A retiring German army, on the other hand, will be far less formidable than a retiring French army, because it has less "devil" in it, because it is made up of men taught to obey in masses, because its intelligence is concentrated in its aristocratic officers, because it is dismayed when it breaks ranks. The German army is everything the Conscriptionists dreamt of making our people; it is, in fact, an army about twenty years behind the requirements of contemporary conditions.

On the Eastern frontier the issue is more doubtful because of the uncertainty of Russian things. The peculiar military strength of Russia, a strength it was not able to display in Manchuria, lies in its vast resources of mounted men. A set invasion of Prussia may be a matter of many weeks, but the raiding possibilities in Eastern Germany are enormous. It is difficult to guess how far the Russian attack will be guided by intelligence, and how far Russia will blunder, but Russia will have to blunder very disastrously indeed before she can be put upon the defensive. A Russian raid is far more likely to threaten Berlin than a German to reach Paris.

Meanwhile there is the struggle on the sea. In that I am prepared for some rude shocks. The Germans have devoted an amount of energy to the creation of an aggressive navy that would have been spent more wisely in consolidating their European position. It is probably a thoroughly good navy, and ship for ship the equal of our own. But the same lack of invention, the same relative uncreativeness that has kept the German behind the Frenchman in things aerial has made him, regardless of his shallow seas, follow our lead in naval matters, and if we have erred, and I believe we have erred, in overrating the importance of the big battleship, the German has at least very obligingly fallen in with our error. The safest, most effective, place for the German fleet at the present time is the Baltic Sea. On this side of the Kiel Canal, unless I overrate the powers of the water-plane, there is no safe harbour for it. If it goes into port anywhere that port can be ruined, and the bottled-up ships can be destroyed at leisure by aerial bombs. So that if they are on this side of the Kiel Canal they must keep the sea and fight, if we let them, before their coal runs short. Battle in the open sea in this case is their only chance. They will fight against odds, and with every prospect of a smashing, albeit we shall certainly have to pay for that victory in ships and men. In the Baltic we shall not be able to get at them without the participation of Denmark, and they may have a considerable use against Russia. But in the end even there mine and aeroplane and destroyer should do their work.

So I reckon that Germany will be held east and west, and that she will get her fleet practically destroyed. We ought also to be able to sweep her shipping off the seas, and lower her flag for ever in Africa and Asia and the Pacific. All the probabilities, it seems to me, point to that. There is no reason why Italy should not stick to her present neutrality, and there is considerable inducement close at hand for both Denmark and Japan to join in, directly they are convinced of the failure of the first big rush on the part of Germany. All these issues will be more or less definitely decided within the next two or three months. By that time I believe German Imperialism will be shattered, and it may be possible to anticipate the end of the armaments phase of European history. France, Italy, England, and all the smaller Powers of Europe are now pacific countries; Russia, after this huge war, will be too exhausted for further adventure; a shattered Germany will be a revolutionary Germany, as sick of uniforms and the Imperialist idea as France was in 1871, as disillusioned about predominance as Bulgaria is to-day. The way will be open at last for all these Western Powers to organise peace. That is why I, with my declared horror of war, have not signed any of these "stop-the-war" appeals and declarations that have appeared in the last few days. Every sword that is drawn against Germany now is a sword drawn for peace.

III
HANDS OFF THE PEOPLE'S FOOD

This is a war-torn article, a convalescent article.

It is characteristic of the cheerful gallantry of the time that after being left for dead on Saturday evening this article should be able, in an only very slightly bandaged condition, to take its place in the firing-line again on Thursday morning.

It was first written late on Friday night; it was written in a mood of righteous excitement, and it was an extremely ineffective article. In the night I could not sleep because of its badness, and because I did so vehemently want it to hit hard and get its effect. I turned out about two o'clock in the morning and redrafted it, and the next day I wrote it all over again differently and carefully, and I think better. In the afternoon it was blown up by the discovery that Mr. Runciman had anticipated its essential idea. He had brought in, and the House had passed through all its stages, a Bill to give the Board of Trade power to requisition and deal with hoarded or reserved food. That was exactly the demand of my article. My article, about to die, saluted this most swift and decisive Government of ours....

Then I perceived that there were still many things to be said about this requisitioning of food. The Board of Trade has got its powers, but apparently they have still to be put into operation. It is extremely desirable that there should be a strong public opinion supporting and watching the exercise of these powers, and that they should be applied at the proper point immediately. The powers Mr. Runciman has secured so rapidly for the Board of Trade have to be put into operation; there must be an equally rapid development of local committees and commandos to carry out his idea. The shortage continues. It is not over. The common people, who are sending their boys so bravely and uncomplainingly to the front, must be relieved at once from the intolerable hardships which a certain section of the prosperous classes, a small section but an actively mischievous section, is causing them. It is a right; not a demand for charity. It is ridiculous to treat the problem in any other way.

So far the poorer English have displayed an amazing and exemplary patience in this crisis, a humility and courage that make one the prouder for being also English. Apart from any failure of employment at the present time, it must be plain to anyone who has watched the present rise of prices and who knows anything either at first hand of poor households or by reading such investigations as those of Mrs. Pember Reeves upon the family budgets of the poor, that the rank and file of our population cannot now be getting enough to eat. They are suffering needless deprivation and also they are suffering needless vexation. And there is no atom of doubt why they are suffering these distresses. It is that pretentious section of the prosperous classes, the section we might hit off with the phrase "automobile-driving villadom," the "Tariff Reform and damn Lloyd George and Keir Hardie" class, the most pampered and least public-spirited of any stratum in the community, which has grabbed at the food; it has given way to an inglorious panic; it has broken ranks and stampeded to the stores and made the one discreditable exception in the splendid spectacle of our national solidarity.

While the attention of all decent English folk has been concentrated upon the preparations for our supreme blow at Prussian predominance in Europe, villadom has been swarming to the shops, buying up the food of the common people, carrying it off in the family car (adorned, of course, with a fluttering little Union Jack); father has given a day from business, mother has helped, even those shiny-headed nuts, the sons, have condescended to assist, and now villadom, feeling a little safer, is ready with the dinner-bell, its characteristic instrument of music, to maffick at the victories it has done its best to spoil. And villadom promoted and distended, villadom in luck, turned millionaire, villadom on a scale that can buy a peerage and write you its thousands-of-pounds cheque for a showy subscription list, has been true to its origins. Lord Maffick, emulating Mr. and Mrs. Maffick, swept his district clean of flour; let the thing go down to history. Lord Maffick now explains that he bought it to distribute among his poorer neighbours—that is going to be the stock excuse of these people—but that sort of buying is just exactly as bad for prices as buying for Lord Maffick's personal interior. The sooner that flour gets out of the houses of Lord Maffick and Horatio Maffick, Esquire, and young Mr. Maffick and the rest of them, and into the houses of their poorer neighbours, the better for them and the country. The greatest danger to England at the present time is neither the German army nor the German fleet, but this morally rotten section of our community.

Now it is no use scolding these people. It is no use appealing to their honour and patriotism. Honour they have none, and their idea of patriotism is to "tax the foreigner," wave Union Jacks, and clamour for the application to England of just that universal compulsory service which leads straight to those crowded, ineffective massacres of common soldiers that are beginning upon the German war-front. Exhortation may sway the ninety-and-nine, but the one mean man in the hundred will spoil the lot. The thing to do now is to get to work at once in every locality, requisitioning all excessive private stores of food or gold coins—they can be settled for after the war—not only the stores of the private food-grabbers, but also the stores of the speculative wholesalers who are holding up prices to the retail shops. Only in that way can the operations of this intolerable little minority be completely checked. Under every county council food committees should be formed at once to report on the necessities of the general mass and conduct inquiries into hoarding and the seizure and distribution of hoards, small and great.

Now this is a public work calling for the most careful and open methods. Food distribution in England is partly in the hands of great systems of syndicated shops and partly still in the hands of one-shop local tradesmen. It is imperative that the brightest light should be kept upon the operations of both small and large provision dealers. The big firms are in the control of men whose business successes have received in many instances marks of the signal favour and trust of our rulers. Lord Devonport, for example, is a peer; Sir Thomas Lipton is a baronet; they are not to be regarded as mere private traders, but as men honoured by association with the hierarchy of our national life on account of their distinguished share in the public food service. It will help them in their quasi-public duties to give them the support of our attention. Are they devoting their enormous economic advantages to keeping prices at a reasonable level, or are these various systems of syndicated provision shops also putting things up against the consumer? With concerted action on the part of these stores the most perfect control of prices is possible everywhere, except in the case of a few out-of-the-way villages. Is it being done? Nobody wants to see the names of Lord Devonport or Sir Thomas Lipton or the various other rich men associated with them in the food supply flourishing about on royal subscription lists at the present time; their work lies closer at hand. What we all want is to feel that they are devoting their utmost resources to the public food service of which they constitute so important a part. Let me say at once that I have every reason to believe they are doing it, and that they are alive to the responsibilities of their positions. But we must keep the limelight on them and on their less honoured and conspicuous fellow-merchants. They are playing as important and vital a part—indeed, they are called upon to play as brave and self-sacrificing a part—as any general at the front. If they fail us it will be worse than the loss of many thousands of men in battle. Let us watch them, and I believe we shall watch them with admiration. But let us watch them. Let us report their movements, ask them to reassure us, chronicle their visits to the Board of Trade.

I will not expatiate upon the possible heroisms of the wholesale provision trade. I do but glance at the possibility of Lord Devonport or Sir Thomas Lipton, after the war, living, financially ruined, but glorious, in a little cottage. "I gave back to the people in their hour of need what I made from them in their hours of plenty," he would say. "I have suffered that thousands might not suffer. It is nothing. Think of the lads who died in Belgium."

By all accounts, the small one-shop provision dealers are behaving extremely well. In my own town of Dunmow I know of two little shopkeepers who have dared to offend important customers rather than fulfil panic orders. They deserve medals. In poor districts many such men are giving credit, eking out, tiding over, and all the time running tremendous risks. Not all heroes are upon the battlefield, and some of the heroes of this war are now fighting gallantly for our land behind grocers' counters and in village general shops, and may end, if not in the burial trench, in the bankruptcy court. Indeed, many of them are already on the verge of bankruptcy. The wholesalers have, I know, in many cases betrayed them, not simply by putting up prices, but by suddenly stopping customary credits, and this last week has seen some dismal nights of sleepless worry in the little bedrooms over the isolated grocery. While we look to the syndicated shops to do their duty, it is of the utmost importance also that we should not permit a massacre of the small tradespeople. A catastrophe to the small shopkeeper at the present time will not only throw a multitude of broken men upon public resources, but leave a gap in the homely give-and-take of back-street and village economies that will not be easily repaired. So that I suggest that the requisitioned stocks of forestalling wholesalers—there ought to be a great bulk of such food-stuff already in the hands of the authorities—shall be sold in the first instance at wholesale prices to the isolated shopkeepers, and not directly to the public. Only in the event of a local failure of duty should the direct course be taken.

It must be remembered that the whole of the present stress for food is an artificial stress due to the vehement selfishness of vulgar-minded prosperous people and to the base cunning of quite exceptional merchants. But under the strange and difficult and planless conditions of to-day quite a few people can start a rush and produce an almost irresistible pressure. The majority of people who have hoarded and forestalled have probably done so very unwillingly, because "others will do it." They would welcome any authoritative action that would enable them to disgorge without feeling that somebody else would instantly snatch what they had surrendered and profit by it. It is for that reason that we must at once organise the commandeering and requisitioning of hoards and reserved goods. The mere threat will probably produce a great relaxation of the situation, but the threat must be carried out to the point of having everything ready as soon as possible to seize and sell and distribute. Until that is done this food crisis will wax and wane, but it will not cease; if we do not carry out Mr. Runciman's initiatives with a certain harsh promptness food trouble will be an intermittent wasting fever in the body politic until the end of the war.

And the business will not be over at the end of the war. The patience of the common people has been astonishing. In countless homes there must have been the extremest worry and misery. But except for a few trivial rows, such as the smashing of the windows of Mr. Moss, at Hitchin, who was probably not a bit to blame, an attack on a bakery somewhere, and some not very bad behaviour in the way of threats and demonstrations on the part of East End Jews, there has been no disorder at all. That is because the people are full of the first solemnity of war, eagerly trustful, and still—well nourished.

At the end unless the more prosperous people pull themselves together it will not be like that.

IV
CONCERNING MR. MAXIMILIAN CRAFT

I find myself enthusiastic for this war against Prussian militarism. We are, I believe, assisting at the end of a vast, intolerable oppression upon civilisation. We are fighting to release Germany and all the world from the superstition that brutality and cynicism are the methods of success, that Imperialism is better than free citizenship and conscripts better soldiers than free men.

And I find another writer who is also being, he declares, patriotically British. Indeed, he waves the Union Jack about to an extent from which my natural modesty recoils. Because you see I am English-cum-Irish, and save for the cross of St. Andrew that flag is mine. To wave it about would, I feel, be just vulgar self-assertion. He, however, is not English. He assumes a variety of names, and some are quite lovely old English names. But his favourite name is Craft, Maximilian Craft—and I understand he was born a Kraft. He shoves himself into the affairs of this country with an extraordinary energy; he takes possession of my Union Jack as if St. George was his father. At present he is advising me very actively how to conduct this war, and telling me exactly what I ought to think about it. He is, in fact, the English equivalent of those professors of Welt Politik who have guided the German mind to its present magnificent display of shrewd, triumphant statecraft. I suspect him of a distant cousinship with Professor Delbruck. And he is urging upon our attention now a magnificent *coup*, with which I will shortly deal.

In appearance Kraft is by no means completely anglicised himself. He is a large-faced creature with enormous long features and a woolly head; he is heavy in build and with a back slightly hunched; he lisps slightly and his manner is either insolently contemptuous or aggressively familiar. He thinks all born Englishmen, as distinguished from the naturalised Englishmen, are also born fools. Always his manner is pervaded by a faint flavour of astonishment at the born foolishness of the born Englishmen. But he thinks their Empire a marvellous accident, a wonderful opportunity—for cleverer people.

So, with a kind of disinterested energy, he has been doing his best to educate Englishmen up to their Imperial opportunities, to show them how to change luck into cunning, take the wall of every other breed and swagger foremost in the world. He cannot understand that English blood does not warm to such ambitions. When he has wealth it is his nature to show it in watch-chains and studs and signet-rings; if he had a wife she would dazzle in diamonds; the furniture of his flat is wonderfully "good," all picked English pieces and worth no end; he thinks it is just dulness and poorness of spirit that disregards these things. He came to England to instruct us in the arts of Empire, when he found that already there was a glut of his kind of wisdom in the German universities. For years until this present outbreak I have followed his career with silent interest rather than affection. And the first thing he undertook to teach us was, I remember, Tariff Reform, "taxing the foreigner." Limitless wealth you get, and you pay nothing. You get a huge national income in imported goods, and also, as your tariff prevents importation, you develop a tremendous internal trade. Two birds (in quite opposite directions) with the same stone. It seemed just plain common sense to him. Anyhow, he felt sure it was good enough for the born English....

He is still a little incredulous of our refusal to accept that delightful idea. Meanwhile his kind have dominated the more docile German intelligence altogether. They have listened to the whisper of Welt Politik, or at least their rulers have attended; they have sown exasperation on every frontier, taken the wall, done all the showily aggressive and successful things. They were the pupils he should have taught. A people at once teachable and spirited. Almost tearfully Kraft has asked us to mark that glorious progress of a once philosophical, civilised, and kindly people. And indeed we have had to mark it and polish our weapons, and with a deepening resentment get more and more weapons, and keep our powder dry, when we would have been far rather occupied with other things.

But amazingly enough we would not listen to his suggestion of universal service. Kraft and his kind believe in numbers. Even the Boer War could not shake his natural aptitude for political arithmetic. He has tried to bring the situation home to us by diagrams, showing us enormous figures, colossal soldiers to represent the German forces and tiny little British men, smaller than the army figures for Bulgaria and for Servia. He does not understand that there can be too many soldiers on a field of battle; he could as soon believe that one could have too much money. And so he thinks the armies of Russia *must* be more powerful than the French. When I deny that superiority—as I do—he simply notes the fact that I am unable to count.

And when it comes to schemes of warfare then a kind of delirium of cunning descends upon Kraft. He is full of devices such as we poor fools cannot invent; sudden attacks without a declaration of war, vast schemes for spy systems and assassin-like disguises, the cowing of a country by the wholesale shooting of uncivil non-combatants, breaches of neutrality, national treacheries, altered dispatches, forged letters, diplomatic lies, a perfect world-organisation of Super-sneaks. Our poor cousin, Michael, the

German, has listened to such wisdom only too meekly. Poor Michael, with his honest blue eyes wonder-lit, has tried his best to be a very devil, and go where Kraft's cousin, Bernhardi, the military "expert," has led him. (So far it has led him into the ditches of Liège and the gorges of the Ardennes and much hunger and dirt and blood.) And Kraft over here has watched with an intolerable envy Berlin lying and bullying and being the very Superman of Welt Politik. He has been talking, writing, praying us to do likewise, to strike suddenly before war was declared at the German fleet, to outrage the neutrality of Denmark, to seize Holland, to do something nationally dishonest and disgraceful. Daily he has raged at our milk and water methods. At times we have seemed to him more like a lot of Woodrow Wilsons than reasonable sane men.

And he is still at it.

Only a few days ago I took up the paper that has at last moved me to the very plain declarations of this article. It was an English daily paper, and Kraft was telling us, as usual, and with his usual despairful sense of our stupidity, how to conduct this war. And what he said was this—that we have to starve Germany—not realising that with her choked railways and her wasted crops Germany may be trusted very rapidly to starve herself—and that, if we do not prevent them, foodstuffs will go into Germany by way of Holland and Italy. So he wants us to begin at once a hostile blockade of Holland and Italy, or better, perhaps, to send each of these innocent and friendly countries an ultimatum forthwith. He wants it done at once, because otherwise the Berlin Krafts, some Delbruck or Bernhardi, or that egregious young statesman, the Crown Prince, may persuade the Prussians to get in their ultimatum first. Then we should have no chance of doing anything internationally idiotic at all, unless, perhaps, we seized a port in Norway. It might be rather a fine thing, he thinks upon reflection, to seize a port in Norway.

Now let us English make it clear, once for all, to the Krafts and other kindred patriotic gentlemen from abroad who are showing us the really artful way to do things, that this is not our way of doing things. Into this war we have gone with clean hands—to end the reign of brutal and artful internationalism for ever. Our hearts are heavy at the task before us, but our intention is grim. We mean to conquer. We are prepared for every disaster, for intolerable stresses, for bankruptcy, for hunger, for anything but defeat. Now that we have begun to fight we will fight if needful until the children die of famine in our homes, we will fight though every ship we have is at the bottom of the sea. We mean to fight this war to its very finish, and that finish we are absolutely resolved must be the end of Kraftism in the world. And we will come out of this war with hands as clean as they are now, unstained by any dirty tricks in field or council chamber, neutralities respected and treaties kept. Then we will reckon once for all with Kraft and with his friends and supporters, the private dealers in armaments, and with all this monstrous, stupid brood of villainy that has brought this vast catastrophe upon the world.

I say this plainly now for myself and for thousands of silent plain men, because the sooner Kraft realises how we feel in this matter the better for him. He betrays at times a remarkable persuasion that at the final settling up of things he will make himself invaluable to us. At diplomacy he knows he shines. Then the lisping whisper has its use, and the studied insolence. Finish the fighting, and then leave it to him. He really believes the born English will. He does not understand in the slightest degree the still passion of our streets. There never was less shouting and less demonstration in England, and never was England so quietly intent. This war is not going to end in diplomacy; it is going to end diplomacy. It is quite a different sort of war from any that have gone before it. At the end there will be no Conference of Europe on the old lines at all, but a Conference of the World. It will be a Conference for Kraft to laugh at. He will run about button-holing people about it; almost spitting in their faces with the eagerness of his derisive whispers. It will conduct its affairs with scandalous publicity and a deliberate simplicity. It will be worse than Woodrow Wilson. And it will make a peace that will put an end to Kraft and the spirit of Kraft and Kraftism and the private armament firms behind him for evermore.

At which I imagine the head of Kraft going down between his shoulders and his large hands going out like the wings of a cherub. "Englishmen! Liberals! Fools! Incurable! How can such things be? It is not how things are done."

It is how they are going to be done if this world is to be worth living in at all after this war. When we fight Berlin, Kraft, we fight *you*.... An absolute end to you. Yes.

V
THE MOST NECESSARY MEASURES IN THE WORLD

In this smash-up of empires and diplomacy, this utter disaster of international politics, certain things which would have seemed ridiculously Utopian a few weeks ago have suddenly become reasonable and practicable. One of these, a thing that would have seemed fantastic until the very moment when we joined issue with Germany and which may now be regarded as a sober possibility, is the absolute abolition throughout the world of the manufacture of weapons for private gain. Whatever may be said of the practicability of national disarmament, there can be no dispute not merely of the possibility but of the supreme necessity of ending for ever the days of private profit in the instruments of death. That is the real enemy. That is the evil thing at the very centre of this trouble.

At the very core of all this evil that has burst at last in world disaster lies this Kruppism, this sordid enormous trade in the instruments of death. It is the closest, most gigantic organisation in the world. Time after time this huge business, with its bought newspapers, its paid spies, its agents, its shareholders, its insane sympathisers, its vast ramification of open and concealed associates, has defeated attempts at pacification, has piled the heap of explosive material higher and higher—the heap that has toppled at last into this bloody welter in Belgium, in which the lives of four great nations are now being torn and tormented and slaughtered and wasted beyond counting, beyond imagining. I dare not picture it—thinking now of who may read.

So long as the unstable peace endured, so long as the Emperor of the Germans and the Krupp concern and the vanities of Prussia hung together, threatening but not assailing the peace of the world, so long as one could dream of holding off the crash and saving lives, so long was it impossible to bring this business to an end or even to propose plainly to bring this business to an end. It was still possible to argue that to be prepared for war was the way to keep the peace. But now everyone knows better. The war has come. Preparation has exploded. Outrageous plunder has passed into outrageous bloodshed. All Europe is in revolt against this evil system. There is no going back now to peace; our men must die, in heaps, in thousands; we cannot delude ourselves with dreams of easy victories; we must all suffer endless miseries and anxieties; scarcely a human affair is there that will not be marred and darkened by this war. Out of it all must come one universal resolve: that this iniquity must be plucked out by the roots. Whatever follies still lie ahead for mankind this folly at least must end. There must be no more buying and selling of guns and warships and war-machines. There must be no more gain in arms. Kings and Kaisers must cease to be the commercial travellers of monstrous armament concerns. With the *Goeben* the Kaiser has made his last sale. Whatever arms the nations think they need they must make for themselves and give to their own subjects. Beyond that there must be no making of weapons in the earth.

This is the clearest common sense. I do not need to argue what is manifest, what every German knows, what every intelligent educated man in the world knows. The Krupp concern and the tawdry Imperialism of Berlin are linked like thief and receiver; the hands of the German princes are dirty with the trade. All over the world statecraft and royalty have been approached and touched and tainted by these vast firms, but it is in Berlin that the corruption has centred, it is from Berlin that the intolerable pressure to arm and still to arm has come, it is at Berlin alone that the evil can be grappled and killed. Before this there was no reaching it. It was useless to dream even of disarmament while these people could still go on making their material uncontrolled, waiting for the moment of national passion, feeding the national mind with fears and suspicions through their subsidised Press. But now there is a new spirit in the world. There are no more fears; the worst evil has come to pass. The ugly hatreds, the nourished misconceptions of an armed peace, begin already to give place to the mutual respect and pity and disillusionment of a universally disastrous war. We can at last deal with Krupps and the kindred firms throughout the world as one general problem, one worldwide accessible evil.

Outside the circle of belligerent States, and the States which, like Denmark, Italy, Rumania, Norway and Sweden, must necessarily be invited to take a share in the final re-settlement of the world's affairs, there are only three systems of Powers which need be considered in this matter, namely, the English and Spanish-speaking Republics of America and China. None of these States is deeply involved in the armaments trade, several of them have every reason to hate a system that has linked the obligation to deal in armaments with every loan. The United States of America is now, more than ever it was, an anti-militarist Power, and it is not too much to say that the Government of the United States of America holds in its hand the power to sanction or prevent this most urgent need of mankind. If the people of the United States will consider and grasp this tremendous question now; if they will make up their minds now that there shall be no more profit made in America or anywhere else upon the face of the earth in raw material; if they will determine to put the vast moral, financial and material influence the States will be able to exercise at the end of this war in the scale against the survival of Kruppism, then it will be possible to finish that vile industry for ever. If, through a failure of courage or imagination, they will not come into this thing, then I fear if it may be done. But I misjudge the United States if, in the end, they abstain from so glorious and congenial an opportunity.

Let me set out the suggestion very plainly. All the plant for the making of war material throughout the world must be taken over by the Government of the State in which it exists; every gun factory, every rifle factory, every dockyard for the building of warships. It may be necessary to compensate the shareholders more or less completely; there may have to be a war indemnity to provide for that, but that is a question of detail. The thing is the conversion everywhere of arms-making into a State monopoly, so that nowhere shall there be a ha'porth of avoidable private gain in it. Then, and then only, will it become possible to arrange for the gradual dismantling of this industry which is destroying humanity, and the reduction of the armed forces of the world to reasonable dimensions. I would carry this suppression down even to the restriction of the manufacture and sale of every sort of gun, pistol, and explosive. They should be made only in Government workshops and sold only in Government shops; there should not be a single rifle, not a Browning pistol, unregistered, unrecorded, and untraceable in the world. But that may be a counsel of perfection. The essential thing is the world suppression of this abominable traffic in the big gear of war, in warships and great guns.

With this corruption cleared out of the way, with the armaments commercial traveller flung down the back-stairs he has haunted for so long—and flung so hard that he will be incapacitated for ever—it will become possible to consider a scheme for the establishment of the peace of the world. Until that is done any such scheme will remain an idle dream. But him disposed of, the way is open for the association of armed nations, determined to stamp out at once every recrudescence of aggressive war. They will not be totally disarmed Powers. It is no good to disarm while any one single Power is still in love with the dream of military glory. It is no good to disarm while the possibility of war fever is still in the human blood. The intelligence of the whole world must watch for febrile symptoms and prepare to allay them. But after this struggle one may count on the pacific intentions of at least the following States: The British Empire, France, Italy, and all the minor States of the north and west; the United States has always been a pacific Power; Japan has had its lesson and is too impoverished for serious hostilities; China has never been aggressive; Germany also, unless this war leads to intolerable insults and humiliations for the German spirit, will be war-sick. The Spanish and Portuguese-speaking Republics of

America are too busy developing materially to dream of war on the modern scale, and the same may presently be true of the Greek, Latin and Slav communities of south-east Europe if, as I hope and believe, this war leads to the rational rearrangement of the Austro-Hungarian Empire. 1915 will indeed find this world a strangely tamed and reasonable world.

There is only one doubtful country, Russia, and for my own part I do not believe in the wickedness and I doubt the present power of that stupendous barbaric State. Finland and a renascent Polish kingdom at least will be weight on the side of peace. It will be indeed the phase of supreme opportunity for peace. If there is courage and honesty enough in men, I believe it will be possible to establish a world council for the regulation of armaments as the natural outcome of this war. First, the trade in armaments must be absolutely killed. And then the next supremely important measure to secure the peace of the world is the neutralisation of the sea.

It will lie in the power of England, France, Russia, Italy, Japan and the United States, if Germany and Austria are shattered in this war, to forbid the further building of any more ships of war at all; to persuade, and if need be, to oblige the minor Powers to sell their navies and to refuse the seas to armed ships not under the control of the confederation. To launch an armed ship can be made an invasion of the common territory of the world. This will be an open possibility in 1915. It will remain an open possibility until men recover from the shock of this conflict. As that begins to be forgotten so this will cease to be a possibility again—perhaps for hundreds of years. Already human intelligence and honesty have contrived to keep the great American lakes and the enormous Canadian frontier disarmed for a century. Warlike folly has complained of that, but it has never been strong enough to upset it. What is possible on that scale is possible universally, so soon as the armament trader is put out of mischief. And with the Confederated Peace Powers keeping the seas and guaranteeing the peaceful freedom of the seas to all mankind, treating the transport of armed men and war material, except between one detached part of a State and another, as contraband, and impartially blockading all belligerents, those who know best the significance of the sea power will realise best the reduction in the danger of extensive wars on land.

This is no dream. This is the plain common sense of the present opportunity.

It may be urged that this is a premature discussion, that this war is still undecided. But, indeed, there can be no decision to this war for France and England at any rate but the defeat of Germany, the abandonment of German militarism, the destruction of the German fleet, and the creation of this opportunity. Nothing short of that is tolerable; we must fight on to extinction rather than submit to a dishonouring peace in defeat or to any premature settlement. The fate of the world under triumphant Prussianism and Kruppism for the next two hundred years is not worth discussing. There is no conceivable conclusion to this war but submission at Berlin. There is no reasonable course before us now but to give all our strength for victory and the establishment of victory. The end must be victory or our effacement. What will happen after our effacement is for the Germans to consider.

A war that will merely beat Germany a little and restore the hateful tensions of the last forty years is not worth waging. As an end to all our effort it will be almost as intolerable as defeat. Yet unless a body of definite ideas is formed and promulgated now things may happen so. And so now, while there is yet time, the Liberalism of France and England must speak plainly and make its appeal to the Liberalism of all the world, not to share our war indeed, but to share the great ends for which we are so gladly waging this war. For, indeed, sombrely enough England and France and Belgium and Russia are glad of this day. The age of armed anxiety is over. Whatever betide, it must be an end. And there is no way of making it an end but through these two associated decisions, the abolition of Kruppism and the neutralisation of the sea.

VI
THE NEED OF A NEW MAP OF EUROPE

At the moment of writing the war has not lasted many days, great battles by land and sea alike impend, and yet I find my steadfast anticipation that Prussianism, Bernhardi-ism, the whole theory and practice of the Empire of the Germans, is a rotten and condemned thing, has already strengthened to an absolute conviction. Unforeseen accidents may happen. I say nothing of the sea, but the general and ultimate result seems to me now as certain as the rising of to-morrow's sun. I do not know how much slaughter lies before Europe before Germany realises that she is fool-led and fool-poisoned. I do not know how long the swaggering Prussian officer will be able to drive his crowded men to massacre before they revolt against him, nor do I know how far the inflated vanity of Berlin has made provision for defeat. Germany on the defensive for all we can tell may prove a very stubborn thing, and Russia's strength may be, and I think is, overestimated. All that may delay, but it will not alter the final demonstration that Prussianism, as Mr. Belloc foretold so amazingly, took its mortal wound at the first onset before the trenches of Liège. We begin a new period of history.

It is not Germany that has been defeated; Germany is still an unconquered country. Indeed, now it is a released country. It is a country glorious in history and with a glorious future. But never more after this war has ended will it march to the shout of the Prussian drill sergeant and strive to play bully to the world. The legend of Prussia is exploded. Its appeal was to one coarse criterion, success, and it has failed. Nevermore will the harshness of Berlin overshadow the great and friendly civilisation of Southern and Western Germany. The work before a world in arms is to clean off the Prussian blue from the life and spirit of mankind.

No European Power has any real quarrel with Germany. Our quarrel is with the Empire of the Germans, not with a people but with an idea. Let us in all that follows keep that clearly in our minds. It may be that the German repulse at Liège was but the beginning of a German disaster as great as that of France in 1871. It may be that Germany has no second plan if her first plan fails; that she will go to pieces after her first defeat. It seems to me that this is so—I risk the prophecy, and I would have us prepare ourselves for the temptations of victory. And so to begin with, let us of the liberal faith declare our fixed, unalterable conviction that it will be a sin to dismember Germany or to allow any German-speaking and German-feeling territory to fall under a foreign yoke. Let us English make sure of ourselves in that matter. There may be restorations of alien territory—Polish, French, Danish, Italian, but we have seen enough of racial subjugation now to be sure that we will tolerate no more of it. From the Rhine to East Prussia and from the Baltic to the southern limits of German-speaking Austria, the Germans are one people. Let us begin with the resolution to permit no new bitterness of "conquered territories" to come into existence to disturb the future peace of Europe. Let us see to it that at the ultimate settlement the Germans, however great his overthrow may be, are all left free men.

When the Prussians invaded Luxemburg they tore up the map of Europe. To the redrawing of that map a thousand complex forces will come. There will be much attempted over-reaching in the business and much greed. Few will come to negotiations with simple intentions. In a wrangle all sorts of ugly and stupid things may happen. It is for us English to get a head in that matter, to take counsel with ourselves and determine what is just; it is for us, who are in so many ways detached from and independent of the national passions of the Continent, not to be cunning or politic, but to contrive as unanimous a purpose as possible now, so that we may carry this war to its end with a clear conception of its end, and to use the whole of our strength to make an enduring peace in Europe. That means that we have to re-draw the map so that there shall be, for just as far as we can see ahead, as little cause for warfare among us Western nations as possible. That means that we have to redraw it justly. And very extensively.

Is that an impossible proposal? I think not. There are, indeed, such things as non-irritating frontiers. Witness the frontiers of Canada. Certain boundaries have served in Europe now for the better part of a hundred years, and grow less amenable to disturbance every year. Nobody, for example, wants to use force to readjust the mutual frontiers in Europe of Holland, Belgium, France, Spain, Portugal and Italy, and none of these Powers desire now to acquire the foreign possessions of any other of the group. They are Powers permanently at peace. Will it not be possible now to make so drastic a readjustment as to secure the same practical contentment between all the European Powers? Is not this war that crowning opportunity? It seems to me that in this matter it behoves us to form an opinion sane and definite enough to meet the sudden impulses of belligerent triumph and override the secret counsels of diplomacy. It is a thing to do forthwith. Let us decide what we are going on fighting for, and let us secure it and settle it. It is not an abstract interesting thing to do; it is the duty of every English citizen now to study this problem of the map of Europe, so that we can make an end for ever to that dark game of plots and secret treaties and clap-trap synthetic schemes that has wasted the forces of civilisation (and made the fortunes of the Krupp family) in the last forty years. We are fighting now for a new map of Europe if we are fighting for anything at all. I could imagine that new map of Europe as if it were the flag of the allies who now prepare to press the Germans back towards their proper territory.

In the first place, I suggest that France must recover Lorraine, and that Luxemburg must be linked in closer union with Belgium. Alsace, it seems to me, should be given a choice between France and an entry into the Swiss Confederation. It would possibly choose France. Denmark should have again the distinctly Danish part of her lost provinces restored to her. Trieste and Trent, and perhaps also Pola, should be restored to Italy. This will re-unite several severed fragments of peoples to their more congenial associates. But these are minor changes compared with the new developments that are now, in some form, inevitable in the East of Europe, and for those we have to nerve our imaginations, if this vast war and waste of men is to end in an enduring peace. The break-up of the Austrian Empire has hung over Europe like a curse for forty years. Let us break it up now and have done with it. What is to become of the non-German regions of Austria-Hungary? And what is to happen upon the Polish frontier of Russia?

First, then, I would suggest that the three fragments of Poland should be reunited, and that the Tsar of Russia should be crowned King of Poland. I propose then we define that as our national intention, that we use all the liberalising influence this present war will give us in Russia to that end. And secondly, I propose that we set before ourselves as our policy the unification of that larger Rumania which includes Transylvania, and the gathering together into a confederation of the Swiss type of all the Servian and quasi-Servian provinces of the Austrian Empire. Let us, as the price greater Servia will pay for its unity, exact the restoration to Bulgaria of any Bulgarian-speaking districts that are now under Servian rule; let us save Scutari from the iniquity of a nose-slashing occupation by Montenegrins and try to effect another Swiss confederation of the residual Bohemian, Slavic and Hungarian fragments. I am convinced that the time has come for the substitution of Swiss associations for the discredited Imperialisms and kingdoms that have made Europe unstable for so long. Every emperor and every king, we now perceive, means a national ambition more organic, concentrated and dangerous than is possible under Republican conditions. Our own peculiar monarchy is the one exception that proves this rule. There is no reason why we should multiply these centres of aggression.

Probably neither Bulgaria nor Servia would miss their kings very keenly, and anyhow, I do not see any need for more of these irritating ambition-pimples upon the fair face of the world. Let us cease to give indigestible princes to the new States that we Schweitzerize. Albania, particularly, with its miscellaneous tribes has certainly no use for monarchy, and the suggestion that has been made for its settlement, as a confederation of small tribal cantons is the only one I have ever heard that seemed to contain a ray of hope for that distracted patch of earth. There is certainly no reason why these people should be exploited by Italy, since Italy can claim a more legitimate gratification. There, in a paragraph, is a sketch of the map of Europe that may emerge from the present struggle. It is my personal idea of our purpose in this war.

Quite manifestly in all these matters I am a fairly ignorant person. Quite manifestly this is crude stuff. And I admit a certain sense of presumptuous absurdity as I sit here before the map of Europe like a carver before a duck and take off a slice here and decide on a cut there. None the less it is what everyone of us has to do. I intend to go on redrawing the map of Europe with every intelligent person I meet. We are all more or less ignorant; it is unfortunate but it does not alter the fact that we cannot escape either decisions or passive acquiescences in these matters. If we do not do our utmost to understand the new map, if we make no decisions, then still cruder things will happen; Europe will blunder into a new set of ugly complications and prepare a still more colossal Armageddon than this that is now going on. No one, I hope, will suggest after this war that we should still leave things to the diplomatists. Yet the alternative to you and me is diplomacy. If you want to see where diplomacy and Welt Politik have landed Europe after forty years of anxiety and armament, you must go and look into the ditches of Liège. These bloody heaps are the mere first samples of the harvest. The only alternative to diplomacy is outspoken intelligence, yours and mine and every articulate person's. We have all of us to undertake this redrawing of the map of Europe, in the measure of our power and capacity. That our power and capacity are unhappily not very considerable does not absolve us. It is for us to secure a lasting settlement of all the European frontiers if we can. If we common intelligent people at large do not secure that, nobody will.

If we have no intentions with regard to the map of Europe, we shall soon be going on with the war for nothing in particular. The Prussian spirit has broken itself beyond repair, and the north coast of France and the integrity of Belgium are saved. All the fighting that is still to come will only be the confirmation and development of that. If we have no further plan before us our task is at an end. If that is all, we may stand aside now with a good conscience and watch a slower war drag to an evil end. Left to herself a victorious Russia is far more likely to help herself to East Prussia and set to work to Russianise its inhabitants than to risk an indigestion of more Poles; Italy may go into Albania and a new conflict with Servia; it is even conceivable that France may be ungenerous. She will have a good excuse for being ungenerous. Meanwhile, German-speaking populations will find themselves under instead of upper dogs in half the provinces of Austria-Hungary; mischievous little kings, with chancellors and national policies and ambitions all complete, will rise and fluctuate and fall upon that slippery soil, and a bloody and embittered Germany, continually stung by the outcries of her subject kindred, will sit down grimly to grow a new generation of soldiers and prepare for her revenge....

That is why I think we liberal English should draw our new map of Europe now, first of all on paper and then upon the face of the earth.

We ought to draw that map now, and propagate the idea of it, and make it our national purpose, and call the intelligence and consciences of the United States and France and Scandinavia to our help. Openly and plainly we ought to discuss and decide and tell the world what we mean to do. The reign of brutality, cynicism, and secretive treachery is shattered in Europe. Over the ruins of the Prussian War-Lordship, reason, public opinion, justice, international good faith and good intentions will be free to come back and rule the destinies of man. But things will not wait for reason and justice, if just and reasonable men have neither energy nor unity.

VII
THE OPPORTUNITY OF LIBERALISM

The opportunity of Liberalism has come at last, an overwhelming opportunity. The age of militarism has rushed to its inevitable and yet surprising climax. The great soldier empire, made for war, which has dominated Europe for forty years has pulled itself up by the roots and flung itself into the struggle for which it was made. Whether it win or lose, it will never put itself back again. All Europe, following that lead, is a-field for war. The good harvests stand neglected, the factories are idle, a thin, uncertain trickle of paper money replaces the chinking flow of commerce; whichever betide, defeat or deadlock, the capitalist military civilisation uproots itself and ends. The war may burn itself out more quickly than those who regard its immensity think, but the war itself is the mere smash of the thing. The reality is the uprooting, the incurable dislocation.

Trying to map and measure that dislocation is rather like one's first effort to think in sun's distances. It is to transfer one's mind to a new and overwhelming scale. Never did any time carry so swift a burthen of change as this time. It is manifest that in a year or so the world of men is going to alter more than it has altered in the last century and a half, more indeed than it ever altered before these last centuries since history began. Think of the mere geographical dislocation. There is scarcely a country in Europe that will not emerge from this struggle with entirely fresh frontiers, sovereign powers will vanish from the map, new sovereign powers will come. In the disorders that are upon us and of which this war itself is the mere preliminary phase in uniform, inevitably there must be social reconstruction. Who can doubt it? Who can doubt the break-up of confidence and usage that is in progress? Plainly you can see famine coming—in France, in Germany, in Russia. Does anyone suppose that those sham efficient Germans have fully worked out the care and feeding of the madly distended hosts they have hurled at France? Does anyone dream that they have reckoned for a check and halt? Does anyone imagine their sanitary arrangements are perfect? There will be pestilence. And can one believe that whatever feats of financial fiction we contrive, *their* financial crash can be staved off, and that the bankers of Hamburg and Frankfort are likely to be shovelling gold next January in a still methodical world? The German State machine has probably already done all that it was ever made to do. It stands now exhausted amidst the turmoil of its consequences. Its mobilization arrangements are said to have been astonishingly complete. Ten million men for and against have been got into the field—with ammunition. Prussian Germany has carried out its arrangements and committed the business to Gott. German foresight has exhausted itself. If Gott fail Germany, I do not believe that Germany has the remotest idea what to do next. For the most part those millions will never get home any more. They will certainly never get back to their work again, because it will have disappeared.

When I think of European statecraft presently trying to put all these things back again I am reminded of a story of a friend whose neighbour tried to cut his throat and then repented. He came round to her with a towel about his neck making peculiar noises. It was a distressing but illuminating experience for her. She was a plucky and resourceful woman, and she did her best. "There was such a lot of it," she said. "I hadn't an idea things were packed so tight in us."

It is characteristic of such times as this—that much in the world, and, more particularly, much in the minds of men, much that has seemed as invincible as the mountains and as deeply rooted as the sea, magically loses its solidity, fades, changes, vanishes. When one looked at the map of Europe a month ago most of the lines of its frontiers seemed almost as stable as the coastlines. Now they waver under one's eyes. When one thought of the heritage of the Crown Prince of Germany, it seemed as fixed as a constellation, and now in a little while it may be worth as little as a bloody rag in the trenches of Liège. In little things as in great, one is suddenly confronted by undreamt-of instabilities. The Reform Club, which has been a cheerful and refreshing trickle of gold to me for years, now yields me reluctantly for my cheque two inartistic pound notes. My other club has ceased the kindly custom of cashing cheques altogether. One is glad that poor Bagehot did not live to see this day. Each day now I marvel to wake and find I have still a banker.... And I perceive too, that if presently my banker dissolved into the rest of this dissolving world—a thing I should have thought an unendurable calamity a month ago—I shall laugh and go on.... Ideas that have ruled life as though they were divine truths are being chased and slaughtered in the streets. The rights of property, for example, the sturdy virtues of individualism, all toleration for the rewards of abstinence, vanished last week suddenly amidst the execrations of mankind upon a hurrying motor-car loaded with packages of sugar and flour. They bolted, leaving Socialism and Collectivism in possession. The State takes over flour mills and the food supply, not merely for military purposes, but for the general welfare of the community. The State controls the railways with a sudden complete disregard of shareholders. There is not even a letter to the *Times* to object. If the State sees fit to keep its hold upon these things for good, or loosens its hold only to improve its grip, I question if there is very much left in the minds of men, even after the mere preliminary sweeping of the last two weeks, to dispute possession. Society as we knew it a year ago has indeed already broken up; it has lost all real cohesion; only the absence of any attraction elsewhere keeps us bunched together. We keep our relative positions because there is nowhither to stampede. Dazed, astonished people fill the streets; and we talk of the national calm. The more intelligent men thrown out of their jobs make for the recruiting offices, because they have nothing else to do; we talk of the magnificent response to Lord Kitchener's appeal. Everybody is offering services. Everybody is looking for someone to tell him what to do. It is not organisation; it is the first phase of dissolution.

I am not writing prophecies now, and I am not "displaying imagination." I am just running as hard as I can by the side of the marching facts, and pointing to them. Institutions and conventions crumble about us, and release to unprecedented power the two sorts of rebel that ordinary times suppress, will and ideas.

The character of the new age that must come out of the catastrophes of this epoch will be no mechanical consequence of inanimate forces. Will and ideas will take a larger part in this *swirl*-ahead than they have even taken in any previous collapse. No doubt the mass of mankind will still pour along the channels of chance, but the desire for a new world of a definite character will be a force, and if it is multitudinously unanimous enough, it may even be a guiding force, in shaping the new time. The common man and base men are scared to docility. Rulers, pomposities, obstructives are suddenly apologetic, helpful, asking for help. This is a time of incalculable plasticity. For the men who know what they want, the moment has come. It is the supreme opportunity, the test or condemnation of constructive liberal thought in the world.

Now what does Liberalism mean to do? It has always been alleged against Liberalism that it is carpingly critical, disorganised, dispersed, impracticable, fractious, readier to "resign" and "rebel" than help. That is the common excuse of all modern autocracies, bureaucracies, and dogmatisms. Are they right? Is Liberal thought in this world-crisis going to present the spectacle of a swarm of little wrangling men swept before the mindless besom of brute accident, or shall we be able in this vast collapse or re-birth of the world, to produce and express ideas that will rule? Has it all been talk? Or has it been planning? Is the new world, in fact, to be shaped by the philosophers or by the Huns?

First, as to peace. Do Liberals realise that now is the time to plan the confederation and collective disarmament of Europe, now is the time to redraw the map of Europe so that there may be no more rankling sores or unsatisfied national ambitions? Are the Liberals as a body going to cry

"Peace! Peace!" and leave the questions alone, or are they going to take hold of them? If Liberalism throughout the world develops no plan of a pacified world until the diplomatists get to work, it will be too late. Peace may come to Europe this winter as swiftly and disastrously as the war.

And next, as to social reconstruction. Do Liberals realise that the individualist capitalist system is helpless *now*? It may be picked up unresistingly. It is stunned. A new economic order may be improvised and probably will in some manner be improvised in the next two or three years. What are the intentions of Liberalism? What will be the contribution of Liberalism? One poor Liberal, I perceive, is possessed, to the exclusion of every other consideration, by the idea that we were not *legally* bound to fight for Belgium. A pretty point, but a petty one. Liberalism is something greater than unfavourable comment on the deeds of active men. Let us set about defining our intentions. Let us borrow a little from the rash vigour of the types that have contrived this disaster. Let us make a truce of our finer feelings and control our dissentient passions. Let us re-draw the map of Europe boldly, as we mean it to be re-drawn, and let us re-plan society as we mean it to be reconstructed. Let us get to work while there is still a little time left to us. Or while our futile fine intelligences are busy, each with its particular exquisitely-felt point, the Northcliffes and the diplomatists, the Welt-Politik whisperers, and the financiers, and militarists, the armaments interests, and the Cossack Tsar, terrified by the inevitable red dawn of leaderless social democracy, by the beginning of the stupendous stampede that will follow this great jar and displacement, will surely contrive some monstrous blundering settlement, and the latter state of this world will be worse than the former.

Now is the opportunity to do fundamental things that will otherwise not get done for hundreds of years. If Liberals throughout the world—and in this matter the Liberalism of America is a stupendous possibility—will insist upon a World conference at the end of this conflict, if they refuse all partial settlements and merely European solutions, they may re-draw every frontier they choose, they may reduce a thousand chafing conflicts of race and language and government to a minimum, and set up a Peace League that will control the globe. The world will be ripe for it. And the world will be ripe, too, for the banishment of the private industry in armaments and all the vast corruption that entails from the earth for ever. It is possible now to make an end to Kruppism. It may never be possible again. Henceforth let us say weapons must be made by the State, and only by the State; there must be no more private profit in blood. That is the second great possibility for Liberalism, linked to the first. And, thirdly, we may turn our present social necessities to the most enduring social reorganization; with an absolute minimum of effort now, we may help to set going methods and machinery that will put the feeding and housing of the population and the administration of the land out of the reach of private greed and selfishness for ever.

VIII
THE LIBERAL FEAR OF RUSSIA

It is evident that there is a very considerable dread of the power and intentions of Russia in this country. It is well that the justification of this dread should be discussed now, for it is likely to affect the attitude of British and American Liberalism very profoundly, both towards the continuation of the war and towards the ultimate settlement.

It is, I believe, an exaggerated dread arising out of our extreme ignorance of Russian realities. English people imagine Russia to be more purposeful than she is, more concentrated, more inimical to Western civilisation. They think of Russian policy as if it were a diabolically clever spider in a dark place. They imagine that the tremendous unification of State and national pride and ambition which has made the German Empire at last insupportable, may presently be repeated upon an altogether more gigantic scale, that Pan-Slavism will take the place of Pan-Germanism, as the ruling aggression of the world.

This is a dread due, I am convinced, to fundamental misconceptions and hasty parallelisms. Russia is not only the vastest country in the world, but the laxest; she is incapable of that tremendous unification. Not for two centuries yet, if ever, will it be necessary for a reasonably united Western Europe to trouble itself, once Prussianism has been disposed of, about the risk of definite aggression from the East. I do not think it will ever have to trouble itself.

Socially and politically, Russia is an entirely unique structure. It is the fashion to talk of Russia as being "in the fourteenth century," or "in the sixteenth century." As a matter of fact, Russia, like everything else, is in the twentieth century, and it is quite impossible to find in any other age a similar social organisation. In bulk, she is barbaric. Between eighty and ninety per cent. of her population is living at a level very little above the level of those agricultural Aryan races who were scattered over Europe before the beginning of written history. It is an illiterate population. It is superstitious in a primitive way, conservative and religious in a primitive way, it is incapable of protecting itself in the ordinary commerce of modern life; against the business enterprise of better educated races it has no weapon but a peasant's poor cunning. It is, indeed, a helpless, unawakened mass. Above these peasants come a few millions of fairly well-educated and actively intelligent people. They are all that corresponds in any way to a Western community such as ours. Either they are officials, clerical or lay, in the great government machine that was consolidated chiefly by Peter the Great to control the souls and bodies of the peasant mass, or they are private persons more or less resentfully entangled in that machine. At the head of this structure, with powers of interference strictly determined by his individual capacity, is that tragic figure, the Tsar. That, briefly, is the composition of Russia, and it is unlike any other State on earth. It will follow laws of its own and have a destiny of its own.

Involved with the affairs of Russia are certain less barbaric States. There is Finland, which is by comparison highly civilised, and Poland, which is not nearly so far in advance of Russia. Both these countries are perpetually uneasy under the blundering pressure of foolish attempts to "Russianize" them. In addition, in the South and East are certain provinces thick with Jews, whom Russia can neither contrive to tolerate nor assimilate, who have no comprehensible projects for the help or reorganisation of the country, and who deafen all the rest of Europe with their bitter, unhelpful tale of grievances, so that it is difficult to realise how local and partial are their wrongs. There is a certain "Russian idea," containing within itself all the factors of failure, inspiring the general policy of this vast amorphous State. It found its completest expression in the works of the now defunct Pobedonostsev, and it pervades the bureaucracy. It is obscurantist, denying the common people education; it is orthodox, forbidding free thought and preferring conformity to ability; it is bureaucratic and autocratic; it is Pan-Slavic, Russianizing, and aggressive. It is this "Russian idea" that Western Liberalism dreads, and, as I want to point out, dreads unreasonably. I do not want to plead that it is not a bad thing; it is a bad thing. I want to point out that, unlike Prussianism, it is not a great danger to the world at large.

So long as this Russian idea, this Russian Toryism, dominates Russian affairs, Russia can never be really formidable either to India, to China, or to the Liberal nations of Western Europe. And whenever she abandons this Toryism and becomes modern and formidable, she will cease to be aggressive. That is my case. While Russia has the will to oppress the world she will never have the power; when she has the power she will cease to have the will. Let me state my reasons for this belief as compactly as possible, because if I am right a number of Liberal-minded people in Great Britain and America and Scandinavia, who may collectively have a very great influence upon the settlement of Europe that will follow this war, are wrong. They may want to bolster up a really dangerous and evil Austria-cum-Germany at the expense of France, Belgium, and subject Slav populations, because of their dread of this Russia which can never be at the same time evil and dangerous.

Now, first let me point out what the Boer War showed, and what this tremendous conflict in Belgium is already enforcing, that the day of the unintelligent common soldier is past; that men who are animated and individualised can, under modern conditions, fight better than men who are unintelligent and obedient. Soldiering is becoming more specialised. It is calling for the intelligent handling of weapons so elaborate and destructive that great masses of men in the field are an encumbrance rather than a power. Battles must spread out, and leading give place to individual initiative. Consequently Russia can only become powerful enough to overcome any highly civilised European country by raising its own average of education and initiative, and this it can do only by abandoning its obscurantist methods, by *liberalising* upon the Western European model. That is to say, it will have to teach its population to read, to multiply its schools, and increase its universities; and that will make an entirely different Russia from this one we fear. It involves a relaxation of the grip of orthodoxy, an alteration of the intellectual outlook of officialdom, an abandonment of quasi-religious autocracy—in short, the complete abandonment of the "Russian idea" as we know it. And it means also a great development of local self-consciousness. Russia seems homogeneous now, because in the mass it is so ignorant as to be unaware of its differences; but an educated Russia means a Russia in which Ruthenian and Great Russian, Lett and Tartar will be mutually critical and aware of one another. The existing Russian idea will need to give place to an entirely more democratic, tolerant, and cosmopolitan idea of Russia as a whole, if Russia is to merge from its barbarism and remain united. There is no cheap "Deutschland, Deutschland über alles" sentiment ready-made to hand. National quality is against it. Patience under patriotism is a German weakness. Russians could no more go on singing and singing, "Russia, Russia over all," than Englishmen could go on singing "Rule, Britannia." It would bore them. The temperament of none of the Russian peoples justifies the belief that they will repeat on a larger scale even as much docility as the Germans have shown under the Prussians. No one who has seen the Russians, who has had opportunities of comparing Berlin with St. Petersburg or Moscow, or who knows anything of Russian art or Russian literature, will imagine this naturally wise, humorous, and impatient people reduplicating the self-conscious drill-dulled, soulless culture of Germany, or the political vulgarities of Potsdam. This is a terrible world, I admit, but Prussianism is the sort of thing that does not happen twice.

Russia is substantially barbaric. Who can deny it? State-stuff rather than a State. But people in Western Europe are constantly writing of Russia and the Russians as though the qualities natural to barbarism were qualities inherent in the Russian blood. Russia massacres, sometimes even with official connivance. But Russia in all its history has no massacres so abominable as we gentle English were guilty of in Ireland in the sixteenth and seventeenth centuries. Russia, too, "Russianizes," sometimes clumsily, sometimes rather successfully. But Germany has sought to Germanise—in Bohemia and Poland, for instance, with conspicuous violence and failure. We "Anglicised" Ireland. These forcible efforts to create uniformity are natural to a phase of social and political development, from which no people on earth have yet fully emerged. And if we set ourselves now to create a reunited Poland under the Russian crown, if we bring all the great influence of the Western Powers to bear upon the side of the liberalising forces in Finland, if we do not try to thwart and stifle Russia by closing her legitimate outlet into the Mediterranean, we shall do infinitely more for human happiness than if we distrust her, check her, and force her back upon the barbarism from which, with a sort of blind pathetic wisdom, she seeks to emerge.

It is unfortunate for Russia that she has come into conspicuous conflict with the Jews. She has certainly treated them no worse than she has treated her own people, and she has treated them less atrociously than they were treated in England during the Middle Ages. The Jews by their particularism invite the resentment of all uncultivated humanity. Civilisation and not revolt emancipates them. And while Russian reverses will throw back her civilisation and intensify the sufferings of all her subject Jews, Russian success in this alliance will inevitably spell Westernisation, progress, and amelioration for them. But unhappily this does not seem to be patent to many Jewish minds. They have been embittered by their wrongs, and, in the English and still more in the American Press, a heavy weight of grievance against Russia finds voice, and distorts the issue of this. While we are still only in the opening phase of this struggle for life against the Prussianised German Empire, this struggle to escape from the militarism that has been slowly strangling civilisation, it is a huge misfortune that this racial resentment, which, great as it is, is still a little thing beside the world issues involved, should break the united front of western civilisation, and that the confidence of Russia should be threatened, as it is threatened now by doubt and disparagement in the Press. We are not so sure of victory that we can estrange an ally. We have to make up our minds to see all Poland reunited under the Russian Crown, and if the Turks choose to play a foolish part, it is not for us to quarrel now about the fate of Constantinople. The Allies are not to be tempted into a quarrel about Constantinople. The balance of power in the Balkans, that is to say, incessant intrigue between Austria and Russia, has arrested the civilisation of South-eastern Europe for a century. Let it topple. An unchallenged Russia will be a wholesome check, and no great danger for the new greater Servia and the new greater Rumania and the enlarged and restored Bulgaria this war renders possible.

One civilised country only does Russia really "threaten," and that country is Sweden. Sweden has a vast wealth of coal and iron within reach of Russia's hand. And I confess I watch Scandinavia with a certain terror during these days. Sweden is the only European country in which there is a pro-German militarist party, and she may be tempted—I do not know how strongly she may not have been tempted already—to drag herself and Norway into this struggle on the German side. If she does, our Government will be not a little to blame for not having given her, and induced Russia to give her, the strongest joint assurances and guarantees of her integrity for ever. But if the Scandinavian countries abstain from any participation in this present war, then I do not see what is to prevent us and France and Russia from making the most public, definite, and binding declaration of our common interest in Sweden's integrity and our common determination to preserve it.

Beyond that, I see no danger to civilisation in Russia anywhere—at least, no danger so considerable as the Kaiser-Krupp power we fight to finish. This war, even if it brings us the utmost success, will still leave Russia face to face with a united and chastened Germany. For it must be remembered that the downfall of Prussianism and the break-up of the Austro-Hungarian Empire, will leave German Germany not smaller but larger than she is now. To India, decently governed and guarded, with an educational level higher than her own, and three times her gross population, Russia can only be dangerous through the grossest misgovernment on our part, and her powers of intervention in China will be restricted for many years. But all our powers of intervention in China will be restricted for many years. A breathing space for Chinese reconstruction is one of the most immediate and least equivocal blessings of this war. Unless the Chinese are unteachable—and only stupid people suppose them a stupid race—the China of 1934 will not be a China for either us or Russia to meddle with. So where in all the world is this danger from Russia?

The danger of a Krupp-cum-Kaiser dominance of the whole world, on the other hand, is immediate. Defeat, or even a partial victory for the Allies, means nothing less than that.

IX
AN APPEAL TO THE AMERICAN PEOPLE

This appeal comes to you from England at war, and it is addressed to you because upon your nation rests the issue of this conflict. The influence of your States upon its nature and duration must needs be enormous, and at its ending you may play a part such as no nation has ever played since the world began.

For it rests with you to establish and secure or to refuse to establish and secure the permanent peace of the world, the final ending of war.

This appeal comes to you from England, but it is no appeal to ancient associations or racial affinities. Your common language is indeed English, but your nation has long since outgrown these early links, the blood of every people in Europe mingles in the unity of your States, and it is to the greatness of your future rather than the accidents of your first beginnings, to the humanity in you, and not to the English and Irish and Scotch and Welsh in you that this appeal is made. Half the world is at war, or on the very verge of war; it is impossible that you should disregard or turn away from this conflict. Unavoidably you have to judge us. Unavoidable is your participation in the ultimate settlement which will make or mar the welfare of mankind for centuries to come. We appeal to you to judge us, to listen patiently to our case, to exert the huge decisive power you hold in the balance not hastily, not heedlessly. For we do not disguise from ourselves that you can shatter all our hopes in this conflict. You are a people more than twice as numerous as we are, and still you are only the beginning of what you are to be, with a clear prospect of expansion that mocks the limits of these little islands, with illimitable and still scarcely tapped sources of wealth and power. You have already come to a stage when a certain magnanimity becomes you in your relation to European affairs.

Now, while you, because of your fortunate position, and because of the sane and brotherly relations that have become a fixed tradition along your northern boundary—we English had a share in securing that—while you live free of the sight and burthen of military preparations, free as it seems for ever, all Europe has for more than half a century bent more and more wearily under a perpetually increasing burthen of armaments. For many years Europe has been an armed camp, with millions of men continually under arms, with the fear of war universally poisoning its life, with its education impoverished, its social development retarded, with everything pinched but its equipment for war. It would be foolish to fix the blame for this state of affairs upon any particular nation; it has grown up, as most great evils grow, quietly, unheeded. One may cast back in history to the Thirty Years' War, to such names as Frederick the Great, Napoleon the First, Napoleon the Third, Bismarck; what does it matter now who began the thing, and which was most to blame? Here it is, and we have to deal with it.

But we English do assert that it is the Government of the German Emperor which has for the last 40 years taken the lead and forced the pace in these matters, which has driven us English to add warship to warship in a pitiless competition to retain that predominance at sea upon which our existence as a free people depends, and which has strained the strength of France almost beyond the pitch of human endurance, so that the education and the welfare of her people have suffered greatly, so that Paris to-day is visibly an impoverished and overtaxed city. And this perpetual fear of the armed strength of Germany has forced upon France alliances and entanglements she would otherwise have avoided.

Let us not attempt to deny the greatness of Germany and of Germany's contributions to science and art and literature and all that is good in human life. But evil influences may overshadow the finest peoples, and it is our case that since the victories of 1871 Germany has been obsessed by the worship of material power and glory and scornful of righteousness; that she has been threatening and overbearing to all the world. There has been a propaganda of cynicism and national roughness, a declared contempt for treaties and pledges, so that all Europe has been uneasy and in fear. And since none of us are saints, and certainly no nations are saintly, we have been resentful; there is not a country in Europe that has not shown itself resentful under this perpetual menace of Germany. And now at last and suddenly the threatened thing has come to pass and Germany is at war.

Because of a murder committed by one of her own subjects Austria made war upon Servia, Russia armed to protect a kindred country, and then with the swiftness of years of premeditation Germany declared war upon Russia and struck at France, striking through the peaceful land of Belgium, a little country we English had pledged ourselves to protect, a little country that had never given Germany the faintest pretext for hostility, and in the hope of finding France unready. Of course, we went to war. If we had not done so, could we English have ever looked the world in the face again?

And it is with scarcely a dissentient voice that England is at war. Never were the British people so unanimous; all Ireland is with us, and the conscience of all the world. And, now this war has begun, we are resolved to put an end to militarism in the world for evermore. We are not fighting to destroy Germany; it is the firm resolve of England to permit no fresh "conquered provinces" to darken the future of Europe. Whatever betide, all German Germany will come out of this war undivided and German still. Her own "conquests" she may have to relinquish, her Poles and other subject peoples, but that is the utmost we shall exact of her. With the accession of Austria, Germany may even come out of this war a larger Germany than at the beginning. We have no hatred of things German and German people. But we are fighting to break this huge fighting machine for ever—this fighting machine which has been such an oppression as no native-born American can dream of, to every other nation in Europe. We are fighting to end Kaiserism and Kruppism for ever and ever. There, shortly and plainly, is our case and our object. Now let us come to the immediate substance of this appeal.

We do not ask you for military help. Keep the peace which it is your unparalleled good fortune to enjoy so securely. But keep it fairly. Remember that we fight now for national existence, and that in the night, even as this is written, within a hundred miles or so of this place, the dark ships feel their way among the floating mines with which the Germans have strewn the North Sea, and our sons and the sons of Belgium and France go side by side, not by the hundred nor by the thousand, but by the hundred thousand, rank after rank, line beyond line—to death. Even as this is written the harvest of death is being reaped. Remember our tragic case. Europe is full of a joyless determination to end this evil for ever; she plunges grimly and sadly into the cruel monstrosities of war, and assuredly there will be little shouting for the victors whichever side may win. At the end we do most firmly believe there will be established a new Europe, a Europe riddened of rankling oppressions, with a free Poland, a free Finland, a free Germany, the Balkans settled, the little nations safe, and peace secure. And it is of supreme importance that we should ask you now—What are you going to do throughout the struggle, and what will you do at the end?

One thing we are told in England that you mean to do, a thing that has moved me to this appeal. For it is not only a strange thing in itself, but it may presently be followed by other similar ideas. Come what may, all the liberal forces in England and France are resolved to respect the freedom of Holland. But the position of Holland is, as you may see in any atlas, a very peculiar one in this war. The Rhine runs along the rear of the long German line as if it were a canal to serve that line with supplies, and then it passes into Holland and so by Rotterdam to the sea. So that it is possible for any neutral power, such as you are, to pour a stream of food supplies and war material by way of Holland almost into the hands of the German combatant line. Even if we win our battles in the field this will enormously diminish our chance of concluding this war. But we shall suffer it; it is within the rights of Holland to victual the Germans in this way, and we cannot prevent it without committing just such another outrage upon the laws of nations as Germany was guilty of in invading Belgium.

And here is where your country comes in. In your harbours lie a great number of big German ships that dare not venture to sea because of our fleet. It is proposed, we are told, to arrange a purchase of these ships by American citizens, to facilitate by special legislation their transfer to your flag, and then to load them with food and war material and send them across the Atlantic and through the narrow seas, seas that at the price of a cruiser and many men we have painfully cleared of German contact mines, to get war prices in Rotterdam and supply our enemies. It is, we confess, a smart thing to do; it will give your people not only huge immediate profits but a mercantile marine at one *coup*; it will certainly prolong the war, and so it will mean the killing and wounding of scores of thousands of young Germans, Englishmen, Frenchmen, and Belgians, who might otherwise have escaped. It is within your legal rights, and we will tell you plainly now that we shall refuse to quarrel with you about it, but we ask you not to be too easily offended if we betray a certain lack of enthusiasm for this idea.

And begun such enterprises as this, what are you going to do for mankind and the ultimate peace of the world? You know that the Tsar has restored the freedom of Finland and promised to re-unite the torn fragments of Poland into a free kingdom, but probably you do not know that he and England have engaged themselves to respect and protect from each other and all the world the autonomy of Norway and Sweden, and of Sweden's vast and tempting stores of mineral wealth close to the Russian boundary. We ask you not to be too cynical about the Tsar's promises, and to be prepared to help us and France and him to see that they become real. And this with regard to Scandinavia, is not only Russia's promise but ours. This is more than a war of armies; it is a great moral upheaval, and you must not judge of the spirit of Europe to-day by the history of her diplomacies. When this war is ended, all Europe will cry for disarmament. Are you going to help then or are you going to thwart that cry? In Europe we shall attempt to extinguish that huge private trade in war material, that "Kruppism" which lies so near the roots of all this monstrous calamity. We cannot do that unless you do it too. Are you prepared to do that? Are you prepared to come into a conference at the end of this war to ensure the peace of the world, or are you going to stand out, make difficulties for us out of our world perplexities, snatch advantages, carp from your infinite security at our Allies, and perhaps in the crisis of our struggle pick a quarrel with us upon some secondary score? Are you indeed going to play the part of a merely numerous little people, a cute trading, excitable people, or are you going to play the part of a great nation in this life and death struggle of the old world civilisations? Are you prepared now to take that lead among the nations to which your greatness and freedom point you? It is not for ourselves we make this appeal to you; it is for the whole future of mankind. And we make it with the more assurance because already your Government has stood for peace and the observation of treaties against base advantages.

Already the wounds of our dead cry out to you.

X
COMMON SENSE AND THE BALKAN STATES

The Balkan States never have been a problem, they have only been a part of a problem. That is why no human being has ever yet produced even a paper solution acceptable to another human being.

The attempt to settle Balkan affairs with the Austro-Hungarian Empire left out of the problem has been like an attempt to deal with a number of hospital cases in which the head and shoulders of one patient, the legs of another, the abdomen of a third had to be disregarded. The bulk of the Servian people and a great mass of the Rumanians were in the Austro-Hungarian system, and it was the Austrian bar to any development of Servia towards the Adriatic that forced that country back into its unhappy conflict with Bulgaria. Now everything has altered. English people need trouble no longer about Austrian susceptibilities, and not merely our interests but our urgent necessities march with the reasonable ambitions of the four Balkan nations.

Let us begin by clearing away a certain amount of nonsense that is said and believed by many good people about two of these States. It is too much the custom to speak and write of Servia and Bulgaria as though they were almost hopelessly barbaric and criminal communities, incapable of participation in the fellowship of European nations. The murder of the late King and Queen of Servia, the assassination of Serajevo, the foolish onslaught of Bulgaria upon Servia that led to the break-up of the Balkan League, and the endless cruelties and barbarities of the warfare in Macedonia, are allowed to weigh too much against the clear need of a reunited Greater Servia, a restored Bulgaria, and the reasonable prospect of a rehabilitated Balkan League.

Now there is no getting over the hard facts of these crimes and cruelties. But they have to be kept in their proper proportion to the tremendous issues now before the world. Let us call in a few figures that will fix the scale. The Servian people number altogether over ten millions, the Rumanians as many, there are more than twenty million Poles, and perhaps seven millions Bulgarians. The Czechs and Slovenes total six or seven millions, the Magyars exceed ten millions, and the Ruthenians still under Austrian control four millions. It is manifest to every reasonable Englishman now that very few of these sixty or seventy million people are likely to be socially and politically happy until they have got themselves disentangled from intimate subjection to alien rulers speaking unfamiliar tongues, and it is equally manifest that until they are reasonably content, the peace of the rest of Europe will remain uncertain. So that it is upon these regions that the peace of England, France, Germany, Russia and Italy rests.

The lives, therefore, of hundreds of millions of people must be affected, for good or evil, by the sane re-mapping and pacification of south-eastern Europe. In that sane re-mapping and pacification we are, in fact, dealing with matters so gigantic that the mere assassination of this person or the murder of that dwindles almost to the vanishing point. It is surely preposterous that the murder of an unwise young King, who subordinated his nation's destinies to a romantic love affair, a murder done, not by a whole nation, not even by a mob, but by less than a hundred officers, who were at least as patriotic as they were cruel, or even the net of conspiracy that killed the Archduke Franz Ferdinand, should stand in the way of the liberation and unity of millions of Serbs who were as innocent of these things as any Wiltshire farmer. All nations have had their criminal and sanguinary phase; the British and American people who profess such a horror of Servia's murders and Bulgaria's massacres must be blankly ignorant of the history of Scotland and Ireland and the darker side of the Red Indians' destiny. If murder conspiracy was hatched in Servia, were there no Fenians in Ireland and America? We English, at any rate, have not let the highly-organised Phœnix Park murders drown the freedom of Ireland for ever, or cause a war with America. The sooner we English and Americans clear our minds of this self-righteous cant against the whole Servian race because of a few horrors inevitable in a state of barbaric disturbance, the sooner we shall be able to help these peoples forward to the freedom and security that alone can make such barbarities impossible. It would be just as reasonable to vow undying hatred and pitiless vengeance against the whole German-speaking race (of seventy millions or so) because of the burning and killing in Liège. Stifled nations, outraged races, are the fortresses of resentful cruelty. This war is no cinematograph melodrama. The deaths of Queen Draga and the Archduke Franz Ferdinand are scarcely in this picture at all. It is not the business of statecraft to avenge the past, but to deal with the possibilities of the present and the hope of the future.

And the open possibility of the present is for us to bring about a revival of the Balkan League, and identify ourselves with the reasonable hopes of these renascent peoples. In that revival England may play an active and directing part. The break-up of the first Balkan League was a deep disappointment to liberal opinion throughout the world; but it was not an irrevocable disaster. The wonder was, indeed, not the rupture but the union. And the rupture itself was very largely due to the thwarting of

Servia, not by her associates, but by Austria. Now Austria is out of consideration. For Rumania and for each of the three Balkan Powers, there is a plain, honourable and reasonable advantage in a common agreement and concerted action with us now. There are manifest compensations for Greece in Epirus and the islands and—we can spare it—Cyprus. For Bulgaria there is a generous rectification of Macedonia. The natural expansion of the two northern States has been already indicated. And should Turkey be foolish and blunder at this crisis, then further very natural and quite desirable readjustments become possible. What holds these States back from concerted action on our side now, is merely the distrusts and enmities left over from the break-up of the first Balkan League. They will not readily trust one another again. But they would trust England. They would sit down now at a conference in which England and Russia and Italy were represented, and to which England and Russia and Italy would bring assurances of a permanent settlement and arrange every detail of their prospective boundaries in a day. They would arrange a peace that would last a century. England could do more than reconcile; she could finance. And the attack upon Vienna and the German rear would then be reinforced immediately by six or seven hundred thousand seasoned soldiers.

Moreover, it is scarcely possible that Italy could refuse to come into this war if a reunited Balkan League did so. With the Servians in Dalmatia it would be scarcely possible to keep the Italians out of Trieste and Fiume, and long before that earnestly awaited Russian avalanche won its way to Berlin, this southern attack might be in Vienna. The time when the scope of this war could be restricted is past long ago, and every fresh soldier who goes into action now shortens the agony of Europe.

But it is not with the immediate military advantages of a Balkan League that I am most concerned. A Balkan League of Peace, for mutual protection, will be an absolute necessity in a regenerated Europe. It is necessary for the tranquillity of the world. It is necessary if the Wiltshire farmer is to herd his sheep in peace; it is necessary if people are to be prosperous and happy in Chicago and Yokohama. Perhaps "Balkan League" is now an insufficiently extensive word, since Rumania is not in the Balkan Peninsula, and Italy must necessarily be involved in any enduring settlement. But it is clear that the settlement of Europe upon liberal lines involves the creation of these various ten-to-twenty-million-people States, none of them powerful enough to be secure alone, but amounting in the aggregate to the greatest power in Europe, and it is equally clear that they must be linked by some common bond and understanding.

There can be no doubt of the very serious complication of all these possibilities by the jerry-built dynastic interests that have been unhappily run up in these new States. It is unfortunate that we have to reckon not only with peoples but kings. Such a monarchy as that of Servia or Bulgaria narrows, personifies, intensifies and misrepresents national feeling. National hatreds and national ambitions can no doubt be at times very malign influences in the world's affairs, but it is the greed and vanities of exceptional monarchs, of the Napoleons and Fredericks the Great, and so forth, that bring these vague, vast feelings to an edge and a crisis. And it will be these same concentrated and over individualised purposes, these little gods of the coin and postage stamp that will stand most in the way of a reasonable Schweitzerisation and pacification of south-eastern Europe. The more clearly this is recognised in Europe now, the less likely are they, the less able will they be to obstruct a sane settlement. On our side, at least, this is a war of nations and not of princes.

It is for that reason that we have to make the discussion of these national arrangements as open and public as we possibly can. This is not a matter for the quiet little deals of the diplomatists. This is no chance for kings. All the civilised peoples of the earth have to form an idea of the general lines upon which a pacific Europe can be established, an idea clear and powerful enough to prevent and override the manœuvres of the chancelleries. The nations themselves have to become the custodians of the common peace. In Italy, indeed, this is already the case. The Italian monarchy is a strong and Liberal monarchy, secure in the confidence of its people; but were it not so, it is a fairly evident fact that no betrayal by its rulers would induce the Italian people to make war upon France in the interests of Austria and Prussia. I doubt, too, if the present King of Bulgaria can afford to blunder again. The world moves steadily away from the phase of Court-centred nationalism to the phase of a collective national purpose. It is for the whole strength of western liberalism to throw itself upon the side of that movement, and in no direction can it make its strength so effective at the present time as in the open and energetic promotion of a new and greater Balkan League.

XI
THE WAR OF THE MIND

All the realities of this war are things of the mind. This is a conflict of cultures, and nothing else in the world. All the world-wide pain and weariness, fear and anxieties, the bloodshed and destruction, the innumerable torn bodies of men and horses, the stench of putrefaction, the misery of hundreds of millions of human beings, the waste of mankind, are but the material consequences of a false philosophy and foolish thinking. We fight not to destroy a nation, but a nest of evil ideas.

We fight because a whole nation has become obsessed by pride, by the cant of cynicism and the vanity of violence, by the evil suggestion of such third-rate writers as Gobineau and Stewart Chamberlain that they were a people of peculiar excellence destined to dominate the earth, by the base offer of advantage in cunning and treachery held out by such men as Delbruck and Bernhardi, by the theatricalism of the Kaiser, and by two stirring songs about Deutschland and the Rhine. These things, interweaving with the tradesmen's activities of the armaments trust and the common vanity and weaknesses of unthinking men, have been sufficient to release disaster—we do not begin to measure the magnitude of the disaster. On the back of it all, spurring it on, are the idea-mongers, the base-spirited writing men, pretentious little professors in frock coats, scribbling colonels. They are the idea. They pointed the way and whispered "Go!" They ride the world now to catastrophe. It is as if God in a moment of wild humour had lent his whirlwinds for an outing to half-a-dozen fleas.

And the real task before mankind is quite beyond the business of the fighting line, the simple awful business of discrediting and discouraging these stupidities by battleship, artillery, rifle and the blood and courage of seven million men. The real task of mankind is to get better sense into the heads of these Germans, and therewith and thereby into the heads of humanity generally, and to end not simply a war, but the idea of war. What printing and writing and talking have done, printing and writing and talking can undo. Let no man be fooled by bulk and matter. Rifles do but kill men, and fresh men are born to follow them. Our business is to kill ideas. The ultimate purpose of this war is propaganda, the destruction of certain beliefs, and the creation of others. It is to this propaganda that reasonable men must address themselves.

And when I write propaganda, I do not for a moment mean the propaganda with which the name of Mr. Norman Angell is associated; this great modern gospel that war does not *pay*. That is indeed the only decent and attractive thing that can still be said for war. Nothing that is really worth having in life does pay. Men live in order that they may pay for the unpaying things. Love does not pay, art does not pay, happiness does not pay, honesty is not the best policy, generosity invites the ingratitude of the mean; what is the good of this huckster's argument? It revolts all honourable men. But war, whether it pay or not, is an atrociously ugly thing, cruel, destroying countless beauties. Who cares whether war pays or does not pay, when one thinks of some obstinate Belgian peasant woman being interrogated and shot by a hectoring German officer, or of the weakly whimpering mess of some poor hovel with little children in it, struck by a shell? Even if war paid twelve-and-a-half per cent. per annum for ever on every pound it cost to wage, would it be any the less a sickening abomination to every decent soul? And, moreover, it is a bore. It is an unendurable bore. War and the preparation for war, the taxes, the drilling, the interference with every free activity, the arrest and stiffening up of life, the obedience to third-rate people in uniform, of which Berlin-struck Germans have been the implacable exponents, have become an unbearable nuisance to all humanity. Neither Belgium nor France nor Britain is fighting now for glory or advantage. I do not believe Russia is doing so; we are all, I believe, fighting in a fury of resentment because at last after years of waste and worry to prevent it, we have been obliged to do so. Our grievance is the grievance of every decent life-loving German, of every German mother and sweetheart who watched her man go off under his incompetent leaders to hardship and mutilations and death. And our propaganda against the Prussian idea has to be no vile argument to the pocket, but an appeal to the common sense and common feeling of humanity. We have to clear the heads of the Germans, and keep the heads of our own people clear about this war. Particularly is there need to dissuade our people against the dream of profit-filching, the "War against German Trade." We have to reiterate over and over again that we fight, resolved that at the end no nationality shall oppress any nationality or language again in Europe for ever, and by way of illustration, we want not those ingenious arrangements of figures that touch the Angell imagination, but photographs of the Kaiser in his glory at a review, and photographs of the long, unintelligent side-long face of the Crown Prince, his son, photographs of that great original Krupp taking his pleasures at Capri and, to set beside these, photographs pitilessly showing men killed and horribly torn upon the battlefield, and men crippled and women and men murdered, and homes burnt and, to the verge of indecency, all the peculiar filthiness of war. And the case that has thus to be stated has to be brought before the minds of the Germans, of Americans, of French people, and English people, of Swedes and Russians and Italians as our common evil, which, though it be at the expense of several Governments, we have to end.

Now, how is this literature to be spread! How are we to reach the common people of the Western European countries with these explanations, these assurances, these suggestions that are necessary for the proper ending of this war? I could wish we had a Government capable of something more articulate than "Wait and see!" a Government that dared confess a national intention to all the world. For what a Government says is audible to all the world. King George, too, has the ear of a thousand million people. If he saw fit to say simply and clearly what it is we fight for and what we seek, his voice would be heard universally, through Germany, through all America. No other voice has such penetration. He is, he has told us, watching the war with interest, but that is not enough; we could have guessed that, knowing his spirit. As a nation, we need expression that shall reach the other side. But our Government is, I fear, one of those that obey necessity; it is only very reluctantly creative; it rests, therefore, with us who, outside all formal government, represent the national will and intention, to take this work into our hands. By means of a propaganda of books, newspaper articles, leaflets, tracts in English, French, German, Dutch, Swedish, Norwegian, Italian, Chinese and Japanese we have to spread this idea, repeat this idea, and *impose upon this war* the idea that this war must end war. We have to create a wide common conception of a re-mapped and pacified Europe, released from the abominable dangers of a private trade in armaments, largely disarmed and pledged to mutual protection. This conception has sprung up in a number of minds, and there have been proposals at once most extraordinary and feasible for its realisation, projects of aeroplanes scattering leaflets across Germany, of armies distributing tracts as they advance, of prisoners of war much afflicted by such literature. These ideas have the absurdity of novelty, but otherwise they are by no means absurd. They will strike many soldiers as being indecent, but the world is in revolt against the standards of soldiering.

Never before has the world seen clearly as it now sees clearly, the *rôle* of thought in the making of war. This new conception carries with it the corollary of an entirely new campaign.

How can we get at the minds of our enemies? How can we make explanation more powerful than armies and fleets? Failing an articulate voice at the head of our country, we must needs look for the resonating appeal we need in other quarters. We look to the Church that takes for its purposes the name of the Prince of Peace. In England, except for the smallest, meekest protest against war, any sort of war, on the part of a handful of Quakers, Christianity is silent. Its universally present organisation speaks no coherent counsels. Its workers for the most part are buried in the loyal manufacture of flannel garments and an inordinate quantity of bed-socks for the wounded. It is an extraordinary thing to go now and look at one's parish church and note the pulpit, the orderly arrangements for the hearers, the proclamations on the doors, to sit awhile on the stone wall about the graves and survey the comfortable vicarage, and to reflect that this is just the local representation of a universally present organisation for the communication of ideas; that all over Europe there are such pulpits, such possibilities of gathering and saying, and that it gathers nothing and has nothing to say. Pacific, patriotic sentiment it utters perhaps, but nothing that anyone can act upon, nothing to draw together, will, and make an end. It is strange to sit alive in the sunshine and realise that, and to think of how tragically that same realisation came to another mind in Europe.

Several things have happened during the past few weeks with the intensest symbolical quality; the murder of Jaurès, for example; but surely nothing has occurred so wonderful and touching as the death of the Pope, that faithful, honest, simple old man. The war and the perplexity of the war darkened his last hours. "Once the Church could have stopped this thing," he said, with a sense of threads missed and controls that have slipped away—it may be with a sense of vivifying help discouraged and refused. The *Tribuna* tells a story that, if not true, is marvellously invented, of the Austrian representative coming to ask him for a blessing on the Austrian arms. He feigned not to hear, or perhaps he did not hear. The Austrian asked again, and again there was silence. Then, at the third request, when he could be silent no longer, he broke out: "No! *Bless peace!*" As the temperature of his weary body rose, his last clear moments were spent in attempts to word telegrams that should have some arresting hold upon the gigantic crash that was coming, and in his last delirium he lamented war and the impotence of the Church....

Intellect without faith is the devil, but faith without intellect is a negligent angel with rusty weapons. This European catastrophe is the tragedy of the weak though righteous Christian will. We begin to see that to be right and indolent, or right and scornfully silent, or right and abstinent from the conflict is to be wrong. Righteousness has need to be as clear and efficient and to do things as sedulously in the right way as any evil doer. There is no meaning in the Christianity of a Christian who is not now a propagandist for peace—who is not now also a politician. There is no faith in the Liberalism that merely carps at the manner of our entanglement in a struggle that must alter all the world for ever. We need not only to call for peace, but to seek and show and organise the way of peace....

One thinks of Governments and the Church and the Press, and then, turning about for some other source of mental control, we recall the organisations, the really quite opulent organisations, that are professedly devoted to the promotion of peace. There is no voice from The Hague. The so-called peace movement in our world has consumed money enough and service enough to be something better than a weak little grumble at the existence of war. What is this movement and its organisations doing now? Ninety-nine people in Europe out of every hundred are complaining of war now. It needs no specially endowed committees to do that. They preach to a converted world. The question is how to end it and prevent its recurrence. But have these specially peace-seeking people ever sought for the secret springs of war, or looked into the powers that war for war, or troubled to learn how to grasp war and subdue it? All Germany is knit by the fighting spirit, and armed beyond the rest of the world. Until the mind of Germany is changed, there can be no safe peace on earth. But that, it seems, does not trouble the professional peace advocate if only he may cry Peace, and live somewhere in comfort, and with the comfortable sense of a superior dissent from the general emotion.

How are we to gather together the wills and understanding of men for the tremendous necessities and opportunities of this time? Thought, speech, persuasion, an incessant appeal for clear intentions, clear statements for the dispelling of suspicion and the abandonment of secrecy and trickery; there is work for every man who writes or talks and has the slightest influence upon another creature. This monstrous conflict in Europe, the slaughtering, the famine, the confusion, the panic and hatred and lying pride, it is all of it real only in the darkness of the mind. At the coming of understanding it will vanish as dreams vanish at awakening. But never will it vanish until understanding has come. It goes on only because we, who are voices, who suggest, who might elucidate and inspire, are ourselves such little scattered creatures that though we strain to the breaking point, we still have no strength to turn on the light that would save us. There have been moments in the last three weeks when life has been a waking nightmare, one of those frozen nightmares when, with salvation within one's reach, one cannot move, and the voice dies in one's throat.